Donostia San Sebastian

everest

Editorial Management: Raquel López Varela
Editorial coordinator: Aizkorri argitaletxea
Text: Jon Obeso Ruíz de Gordoa
Photographs: Sara Santos
Diagrams: Luis Alonso
Cover Design: Francisco A. Morais
Digital Image Processing: David Aller
Cartography: Editorial Everest
Translation: Euro:text

Editorial Everest would like to thank you for purchasing this book. It has been created by an extensive and complete publishing team made up of photographers, illustrators and authors specialised in the field of tourism, together with our modern cartography department. Everest guarantees that the contents of this work were completely up to date at the time of going to press, and we would like to invite you to send us any information that helps us to improve our publications, so that we may always offer QUALITY TOURISM.

Please send your comments to:
Editorial Everest. Dpto. de Turismo
Apartado 339 - 24080 León (Spain)
Or e-mail them to us at: info@everest.es

Carretera León-A Coruña, km 5 - LEÓN
ISBN: 978-84-441-3199-3
Legal Deposit: LE. 340 - 2011
Printed in Spain

EDITORIAL EVERGRÁFICAS, S. L.
Carretera León-A Coruña, km 5
LEÓN (Spain)

www.everest.es
Customer service: 902 123 400

La Concha Bay is the ideal spot for a host of beach activities and water sports, including all types of sailing, paddle surfing or canoeing.

ON THE OTHER SIDE OF THE PYRENEES

"A promontory to the right, a promontory to the left, two gulfs; an isthmus in the middle, a mountain in the sea; and at the foot of the mountain a city. And there you have it: San Sebastian.

The first impression is magical; the second nothing short of thrilling. An ancient lighthouse stands to the left of the promenade. An island in the bay nestling beneath the lighthouse. A convent standing in ruins. A sandy beach. The oxcarts that go down to the beach to unload the vessels laden with iron ore. The Port of San Sebastian is a fascinating tangle of breakwaters.

To the right, Loyola Valley, home to flocks of robins and where the Urumea, a spectacular steel grey river, traces a huge horseshoe...

San Sebastian looks like a city that has been rebuilt, as straight and square as a chessboard".

This is how Victor Hugo described his impression of the city in the summer of 1843, at the start of his chronicles of his travels on the other side of the Pyrenees.

During the 18th century, that "other side" had fuelled the temptation of enlightened minds to minds to intervene in subjugated and superstitious cultures still to be brought under the yoke of civilisation - "Africa begins in the Pyrenees", claimed Dominique Dufour de Pradt. Later, in the 19th century, it fired the traveller's romantic fascination and his quest for adventure in the midst of natural and unspoilt landscapes. "San Sebastián", wrote Hans Christian Andersen in 1863, "nestles picturesquely in a cove of the Bay of Biscay; the rocks that surround it rise up sharply from the bottom of its deep green waters... San Sebastian is a favourite destination with many French people; you can tell that here one is among the descendents of the country's tribes, the formidable Iberians, or, as they are called in their language: *escauldunac*".

The sight of the waves crashing over the walls of Paseo Nuevo, the promenade that runs around Mount Urgull, is one of the greatest natural highlights of San Sebastian.

Below, the new terrace and lookout point next to the Yacht Club, standing close to the port between the seawall and the jetty, is the ideal spot from which to admire the cityscape.

At the eastern end of La Concha Bay, behind the City Hall, numerous pleasure boats and yachts mingle with the odd fishing boat at the port's mooring berths.

Victor Hugo, on the other hand, adopted a more temperate and calmer approach to the adventures to be lived; his was a vision of "ideas and sensations" inspired by everyday life rather than the sublime and the picturesque.

"A mountain in the middle of the sea. The marks left by bombs on every house, the traces of storms on every rock, the traces of fleas on every road; all this is San Sebastian...", wrote the poet after comparing the city with a twenty-six ounce pound of chocolate.

A SEAFARING CITY

The history of San Sebastian has been written by the hand of its unique geography. Its coastal location, dominated by La Concha Bay, flanked by Mount Igueldo and Mount Urgull,

A beach football tournament on La Concha and a trainera boat training session. In the background, Miramar Palace looking out over the bay and the popular Pico del Loro (a nickname attributed to the site of the former Shrine to the Virgen de Loreto, Loreto-pea), a rocky crag that separates La Concha and Ondarreta beaches.

SAN SEBASTIAN

La Concha Bay forms a stunning natural backdrop for the spectacular regattas, which always attract large crowds. Held on the first two Sundays in September, the Bandera de la Concha, a traditional regatta which dates back over a hundred years, is one of the most eagerly awaited events on the sporting calendar and the most important competition on the Cantabrian circuit.

made it the ideal choice for the trading port of the Kingdom of Navarre following the founding of the city in 1180 by Sancho the Wise and until 1200, when Guipuzkoa fell under the domain of Alphonse VIII, turning San Sebastian into a major seaport for the rapidly expanding Kingdom of Castile.

Proof of the demographic and economic importance of this medieval, mainly Gascon-speaking settlement situated at the foot of Mount Urgull lies in the existence of two churches within its boundaries - Santa María and San Vicente - the object of a dispute between Leire Monastery and the Bishop of Pamplona for thirty years.

This seafaring town was the point of departure for the military expeditions heading to reconquer the South (Seville, 1248; Algeciras, 1350) and the French naval campaigns against England during the Hundred Years' War. In times of peace it exported iron and wool from Castile to the cities

Below, a view of the city nestling between its two coves - La Concha and La Zurriola, presided over by mounts Urgull and Ulia respectively.

The Pietá, *a sculpture based on one of the studies by Jorge Oteiza dating between 1953 and 1969 for the frieze on the Shrine of Arantzazu. Measuring 200 x 180 cm, this aluminium sculpture has featured on the wall of the Church of San Vicente, situated in the city's Old Quarter since 1999.*

Next page, a sculpture of Saint Sebastian on the main façade of the Baroque Basilica of Santa María del Coro, on Calle Mayor, also in the Old Quarter.

of the north (England, Flanders and France), from where it also imported numerous goods, including textiles. This trade was regulated by the Consulate of Biscay in the city of Bruges.

The prosperity of this medieval town and the loyalty it showed to the Castilian crown further strengthened its position, leading Henry II in 1376 to declare it "the finest town in Guipuzkoa and truest to our service...".

The unique layout of La Concha Bay – sheltered by the Island of Santa Clara – allowed for the early harbour and its activity to spread from the walls along the waterfront, forming the 'main port'. An second area of anchorage, known as the 'small port, was located in the fishing grounds of Santa Catalina, next to the bridge of the same name on the banks of the Urumea, and was used by river traffic making its way inland. The town's tradesmen set up their businesses between these two ports: mills and winepresses used by the small farms were dotted around the walled settlement, as well as carpenters, shoemakers and blacksmiths' workshops.

A third area of anchorage was situated in Aquende, nestling at the foot of Mount Ulía, today known as San Pedro, and the most suitable for deeper draft vessels.

It was not until the second half of the 15th century that a stone quay was built parallel to Mount Urgull, with its head jutting out towards the sea. Further building work in the 16th century created a curved dock

Through the Sea Gate (Portaletas) on the old city walls, the narrow streets of the evocative Old Quarter run down to the harbour, with its fish market, fishing dock and marina.

La Mota Castle, a National Historic and Artistic Monument since 1921, stands as a testimony to the city's military past. Since 1950, this fortress has been presided over by the monument to the Sacred Heart. Watched over by Mount Urgull, the old quarter and fishing harbour form an intricate pattern of rooftops and masts.

providing greater shelter for vessels. Other additions included the outer seawall and new mooring berths. These constructions were much admired in their day for the speed and skill with which they were completed. Yet by the 18th century, the port was already proving too small to keep up with the constant coming and going of vessels, although it was not until 1847 that further extension work and improvements were carried out. These included a new outer seawall that enclosed the bay and an inner dock running parallel to the walls, as well as alteration work and deepening of the draft of the existing ones.
The wall that surrounded the town nestling at the foot of Mount Urgull, battered by the Cantabrian Sea had long been an object of attention; in 1311 King Ferdinand IV set aside three thousand *maradevís* a year

No one can claim to really know this city without a first-hand experience of its many 'rituals'. Touring the bars and taverns, sampling the mouth-watering 'pintxos' that line each bar, accompanied by a selection of fine wines, is a gastronomic and social experience not to be missed. Below, A Fuego Negro.

Above, fish ready for auction at the port fish market. Below, the new Cánovas space, the forecourt to La Bretxa Market in the Old Quarter, between the Pescadería commercial building and the market, designed by architect Javier Solano.

The city's districts spread out from the banks of the River Urumea. To the right, the Old Quarter and romantic district with Amara in the background. On the left-hand side, the Egia y Gros quarter, site of the Kursaal Palace, with La Zurriola Beach at the mouth of the Urumea.

The Naval Museum, located in the port, tells the city's maritime history from the 18th century onwards.

from the sea tithes for its conservation. Inside the walls, the local residents lived under the constant threat of fire: indeed, San Sebastian suffered no less than half a dozen blazes between the total destruction of the town in 1278 and the equally devastating fire of 1489. Yet there were others during the Modern

Age, the last of which occurred in 1813, started by the liberating Portuguese and British forces, who, jealous of the city's power and under the pretext of freeing it from the French, had the unhappy idea of razing it to the ground.

THE MILITARY CITY

Major shifts on the international scene - with Castile and Aragón embarking on a long period of hostilities with France and Portugal -, combined with its strategic border location (San Sebastian was known as "the key to France"), made the town a prime target for numerous sieges. Following the siege of 1476 in response to the aid San Sebastian gave the Crown in putting down the uprising of a number of coastal towns (Vivero, Pontevedra and Bayona) in favour of Alphonse V of Portugal, the Catholic Monarchs commissioned the reinforcing of the wall, "adding towers and securing the town to create a fortified enclosure of ramparts and battlements", thus providing it with a new role: that of a military stronghold.
Furthermore, and following the devastating fire of 1489, the Monarchs ordered the reconstruction of the city in stone, heaping further privileges upon it. The 16th and 17th centuries saw a series of campaigns in which San Sebastian served the interests of the Crown against France. During this period, the old medieval fortifications, a simple square surrounding Mount Urgull, with its six gateways and topped by La Mota Castle, were hastily reinforced due to the numerous sieges the town was subjected to. The perimeter walls were widened, raised and reinforced with four towers. Particularly worthy of mention due to the

The emblematic Calle 31 de Agosto, in the historic quarter, commemorates the storming and burning of the old city in 1813 and the fall of the French defences at the hands of the English and Portuguese troops. Accompanied by candles on the balconies and façades and an evocative silence broken only by the thunderous beating of the drums, this ceremony is a truly moving commemoration of the events that took place on this date.

On 20th January, the Day of Saint Sebastian, the raising and lowering of the flag by the Sociedad Gaztelubide and the Unión Artesana respectively in Plaza de la Constitución, at the heart of the Old Quarter, mark the start and finish of twenty-four hours of celebrations, accompanied by the imposing sound of beating drums.

sophisticated techniques used at the time of its construction (1520) - is the Imperial Tower, which faced inland, protecting the southern face, noted for its pentagonal shape and exceptional height and thickness. The castle also boasted a number of artillery platforms looking out over the port of La Concha and the mouth of the Urumea, connected by a new wall separating the castle from the town. The site also included bastions, hornwork and other fortifications, transforming the town into a military stronghold.

Although this new status would earn it the title of a 'Nobel and Loyal' city, conferred by the grace of King Charles V, as well as its city charter, granted in 1662 by Philip IV, honours that were further added to in 1699 by Charles II, who declared it a 'Very Noble and Very Loyal City', the parasitic cost of war resulting from the construction of the new fortifications and the upkeep of the garrisons stationed there were a major drain on the city's economic resources.

San Sebastian was forced to witness its decline as a trading power. The major commercial traffic lines had moved to Bilbao and the Port of Pasajes became a naval base for the Cantabria Squadron. This situation would worsen from 1573 onwards, following Seville's monopoly on trade with America.

In addition to the gastronomic societies, children play a key role in the celebrations to commemorate the Day of Saint Sebastian. Alderdi Eder Park, facing the City Hall, is the point of departure for the children's drum parade.

The next double page shows the Fair of Saint Thomas, held on 21 December in Plaza de la Constitución, where visitors can sample the delicious local fare.

These circumstances would force the city to alter its commercial policies. The result was the creation of the Port Authority - known as the 'Consulate' - and Trading House in 1682 and the Real Compañía Guipuzcoana de Caracas in 1727.

In 1717, the city was occupied by the French troops led by the Duke of Berwick. The city would once again be taken in 1807 during the Peninsular War, this time by Napoleon's troops. This period of conflict was brought to a close by the attack of the Duke of Wellington's British and Portuguese troops under the command of Sir Thomas Graham in 1813, when the city was looted and razed to the ground. Only two churches (Santa María and San Vicente), the Consulate Tower - since 1991 home to the Naval Museum - San Telmo - today the Municipal Museum - and a mere thirty-six houses, the majority on the street at the time called *31 de Agosto,*

were left standing. A document dated just a month after the assault gives a clear idea of the magnitude of this tragedy, declaring that "Today the city has a mere 300 inhabitants".
The city's precarious situation once again forced it to reinvent itself. In the wake of the devastation, the city's representatives met in Zubieta - situated on the outskirts - in order to tackle the disaster that had befallen them. They decided to take on the mammoth task of persuading the residents to stay and rebuild the city.
The new urban vision is reflected in the Neo-Classical designs of Pedro Manuel de Ugartemendía, who would create an enlightened city rising up from the ruins of the old. He is responsible for the construction of the new Plaza de la Constitución (1817-1828) - on the site of the previous one – with the building, designed by

Recent extension and alteration work to the former artillery barracks that in the 16th century were converted into a Dominican convent and a unique example of Isabelline architecture in the province of Guipúzcoa, has turned the San Telmo Museum into an outstanding centre of heritage and culture.

View of La Concha Beach from Mount Urgull. Below, the Old Quarter stretches out in a maze of picturesque streets, fascinating shops and countless restaurants and bars. An irresistible invitation to explore these charming spots, steeped in history.

Silvestre Pérez, that until 1945 would house the City Hall, and later the Municipal Library, occupying one side of the square, in the style of many of Spain's *Plazas Mayores*. The numbers on the balconies of the houses overlooking the square are proof that it was once used as a bullring.
Today, large crowds of local residents gather in the square on 20 January, the Day of San Sebastian, answering the call of the drums that play the city's march – composed by Raimundo Sarrieguie, with lyrics by Serfaín Baroja – in a parody of the Napoleonic occupation during the Peninsular War (1808-1812). It is also the site of the Santo Tomás Market, held on 21 December, a lively mix of farmyard animals, *txistorra* cured sausages, cider and *talo* corn flour tortillas.
Once the reconstruction work was complete, this former powerful medieval trading port and modern stronghold city took its first steps towards the creation of the new San Sebastian that has lasted until the current time.
Through the creation of new districts, the impeccable design of the streets and buildings that line the bay and the banks of the River Urumea, the city of San Sebastian would, in the words of Jorge de Vigo, writing in 1957, "gradually lose its original appearance of a primitive fishing town first and walled enclosure second, to become an outstanding summer resort".

The start of the Cortazar-Goicoa modern district, running between the boulevard and Avenida de la Libertad, marks the romantic area, where visitors can relax and browse around the countless stores and enjoy a pleasant stroll through the Alderdi Eder Park facing the bay and the Plaza Guipúzcoa Park in the centre.

San Sebastian is tailor-made for urbanites. Exploring the city is the best way to get your bearings.

THE SPA CITY

During the course of the 19th century San Sebastian consolidated its position as a liberal city, at odds with the rest of the province, and its permanent capital from 1852 onwards. Following the demolition of the wall in 1863, the city embarked on a period of natural expansion and growth, spreading out over the flat areas beneath the foothills and making its way along the coast and up the banks of the Urumea.

From the port, chartered motor launches carry passengers to the Island of Santa Clara. Leisure options also include a boat trip around Txingudi Bay, along the River Bidasoa, or the Mount Jaizkibel coast, that links Pasajes de San Juan with Hondarribia.

This busy boulevard is an ideal meeting spot, or for indulging in a little people-watching, or even reading the press at one of the street cafés. It's a popular first stop for couples and groups of friends on a great night out in San Sebastian.
Next page, the marble weather and astronomy temple in Plaza Guipúzcoa Park.

In 1864 the architect Cortázar received approval to create a district situated between the boulevard that joins the old and new towns, conceived by Vitoriano Martón Saracíbar – and the famous Plaza del Centenario, based on an isotropic model of identical blocks surrounding a central courtyard, typical of 19th century architecture and imitating the style of Barcelona (Cerdá, 1859) and Madrid (Castro, 1860). In addition to this Classicist Greek-style model, Cortázar also envisioned a city divided into three sections, in keeping with the class and social condition of its inhabitants. Unlike Hipodamo de Mileto, who, in his conception of an essentially functional city, had arranged the urban space in accordance with its trades and professions: craftsmen, farmers and soldiers, in his project entitled *Porvenir* ('The Future'), Cortázar envisioned the following layout: "The first of the spaces – Avenida de la Libertad and Plaza Guipúzcoa, situated in the centre of the city and sheltered from the wind – is for the city's wealthiest residents; the second - facing the bay – for summer visitors and bathers; and the third – the districts of San Martín and Amara, which, despite the fact that the views are not so fine and the population density is higher, is more sheltered from the strong winds -, is for the trade and working classes".

Barrenetxe

The carefully studied disorder of Plaza Guipúzcoa Park, with its meteorological artefacts and astronomy devices, the flower clock, the botanical species and the duck pond crossed by a small wooden bridge, makes this a haven of tranquillity and fantasy.

The tree-lined walks that run along the shores of the Urumea tidal estuary are the perfect choice for some quiet contemplation. The photography shows Los Fueros Walk, facing the Francia Walk, with the María Cristina Bridge and Equitativa Building in the background.

Cortázar's vision was, in his own words, the result of the city's so-called "natural and historical circumstances", and his attempt to preserve its character as a city of tradesmen and merchants. At the same time, he also revealed a vision that overlooked somewhat the delights of the 'matchless backdrop' that the city gradually submitted to over the years- namely the landscape, the wind, the salt water and the tides. Perhaps he had been forewarned by Andrea Palladio, who wrote that "Great care must be taken to ensure that cities do not face the wind directly, as this will lead it to whip violently and furiously through them. For questions of health, they must be broken, gentle, purged and weary...".

In this sense, designing a cityscape that would meet the commercial demands of an emerging tourist industry and would recreate the spirit of cities such as Antwerp, Nice or Biarritz, would fall to the later contributions of José Goicoa. Responsible for creating many of modern day San Sebastian's most

ekp

Left, the marina.

Alderdi Eder Park, opposite the City Hall, with its neat rows of palm and tamarisk trees. An ideal spot for leisure and recreation facing La Concha Bay, at the centre of this park stands a bronze monument by Aitor Mendizabal Ituarte entitled Memory, in honour of all the victims of terrorism.

Following on from the Amara-Osinaga district, the city finds its natural path for growth, following the Urumea into Riberas de Loyola. In the foreground, the Iesu Church, the work of Rafael Moneo.

The Cathedral of El Buen Pastor, noted for its striking vertical structure. The slender bell tower rising above the main portico is inspired by the spires of Cologne Cathedral. Its magnificent organ is one of the largest in Europe.

outstanding hallmarks which, taking the sense of "acceptance and modulation" of the original layout as the basis, he conferred an air of elegance and distinction on the city, adding to Cortázar's Classicist project, an eclecticism worthy of the magnificent architecture of France.
The extension of a number of streets, the channelling of the Urumea – allowing for the creation of new urban spaces such as Paseo de Francia, lined with noble houses and scattered with touches worthy of Paris – such as Alderdi Eder Park lined with its spectacular and much-loved tamarisk trees –, and Paseo de La Concha were just a few of the additions to the new cityscape. Nor must we forget the Neo-Gothic Cathedral of El Buen Pastor (1897), designed by Manuel Echave and located in the heart of the Ensanche district, aligned with the Church of Santa María.

1907
CORREOS
CORREOS

The Post Office, at the far end of Plaza del Buen Pastor, designed by the architect Aguirrebengoa and built in 1906. The ornamental façade reminds us that this was once the sight of the School of Arts and Crafts. The attic windows reflect a certain French influence.

The Koldo Mitxelena cultural centre not only boasts a vast library area, housing the collection of the Guipúzcoa County Council, but also organises an extensive programme of cultural events in its two exhibition rooms and lecture theatre.

José Goicoa was responsible for a number of monumental buildings scattered around the city. These include Goikoa Palace, the School of Arts and Crafts (today the Post Office), the building housing the Koldo Mitxelena Cultural Centre, the Infant School on Paseo del Árbol de Gernika, the Tobacco Factory, the old military hospital, the former *Kursaal*, Polloe Cemetery, the Schools of Zuloaga, in the Old Quarter or the Church of San Ignacio in Gros and Miramar Palace.

In contrast to this sedate and carefully-constructed beauty, the more spontaneous and functional side to San Sebastian can be seen to the west and east in the districts known as El Antiguo and Gros; a fascinating social and architectural melting pot and home to small factories and workshops.

Undoubtedly some of the most outstanding examples of the city's built heritage are its bridges. From the mouth of the Urumea tidal estuary we find a succession of bridges: Kursaal or Zurriola (Ribera, 1921);

In the district known as Egia, the former tobacco factory, today converted into the International Centre for Contemporary Culture, hosts events related to new art forms: film, television and audiovisuals. Tabakalera, now a factory of images. Below, Miramar Palace.

Mundaiz Bridge offers an efficient solution for the city's traffic, whilst adding a note of serene modernity to the city's riverscape.

Santa Catalina (A. Cortázar, 1872) or María Cristina (Ribera y Zapata, 1905), built in the style of the Pont Alexandre III in Paris. In sharp contrast to these, there is a fourth, single-span bridge known as Mundáiz (Fernández Ordóñez, 2000), which stands out for its simple design, free from ornamentation. Work is currently being completed on a fifth bridge, Lehendakari José Antonio Aguirre, which connects the district of Amara with the right bank of the Urumea.

The love of all things French is reflected in the commissions to engineers such as C.A. Letourneur for the construction of the North Station (1864), or Biarez, one of Eiffel's disciples, for the first alterations, carried out in 1881. The landscaping of the city's best-known park, Alderdi Eder, Plaza Guipúzcoa and the grounds of the palaces of Miramar, Aiete and Cristina-Enea – the latter of these donated by the Duke of Mandas to the city in memory of his wife, on the strict condition that it should not be altered in any way – was entrusted to the exquisite taste of royal gardener Pierre Ducasse.

Plaza Guipúzcoa, a leafy shady spot in the city centre, conserves its romantic air. "Everything there", wrote Dunixi in *Mi pueblo, ayer*, "is proportion, calm and harmony. What it may lack in comparison with a grander, larger square, it amply makes up for with its elegant and patrician park". The façade of the main

This city boasts numerous landmarks and symbols. Examples include the futuristic and expressionist style streetlamps that line La Zurriola Bridge, the stately obelisks that flank María Cristina Bridge or the ethereal light that radiates from the Moneo cubes.

Cristina-Enea Park, in the district of Egia, spreads out over 95,000 square metres and is home to a host of plant and shrub species, making it one of the city's most important green lungs. Indeed, together with its natural beauty, the city's parks and gardens form its most important heritage.

Guipúzcoa County Hall, standing in Plaza Guipúzcoa Park, built in an eclectic, Neo-Baroque style.

building, the Provincial Council House, proudly displays the busts of the Basque Country's most famous seamen: Elcano, Urdaneta, Legazpi, Blas de Lezo and Antonio de Oquendo.
Aiete Palace (1878), designed in the Neo-Classical style by the French Architect Adolfo Ombrecht and commissioned by the Duke and Duchess of Bailén, stands on an ancient section of the Pilgrims' Route to Santiago, and was the headquarters of the Duke of Berwick during the 1719 siege of San Sebastian and a place of rest and relaxation for dictators and kings. Indeed, continuing the tradition of the Spanish royal courts, General Franco used it as his summer residence from 1939 until a year before his death. He was preceded by several monarchs: Queen Isabella II, who wished to be near the sea in order to cure her skin infection, Alphonse XII and Maria Christina - named honorary mayoress of the city - and Alphonse XIII. They used it between 1887 and 1893, until Miramar Palace, overlooking the bay between La Concha and Ondarreta, which would be the Court's residence until 1929, the year of the Regent's death.

Miramar Palace, reminiscent of an English country house, is a Gothic style building designed by the English architect Selden Wornum. Today it is home to the University of the Basque Country's summer courses and 'Musikene', the autonomous community's School of Music, as well as a number of other services and institutions, such as the Society of Basque Studies.

In the early 20th century, the presence of the Court attracted many members of the European aristocracy to the city, as well as the wealthy bourgeoisie, drawn by their desire to copy the habits and customs of the upper classes. They came in search of pleasure, in an attempt to put aside the horrors and suffering of the First World War, immersing themselves in the delights of Paris fashions, therapeutic sea bathing, casinos, dances and concerts, horse races and bullfights – held in the former Chofre Bullring, in Gros -, and the amusement parks (Igueldo, 1912). A feverish, frenzied world, dazzled by the image of progress

Perched on one of the city hills, the stately Aiete Palace is famed for its botanical and water species, its cave and artificial waterfall. Below, the abstract Culture Centre and Institute for Human Rights, the House of Peace.

The International Fireworks Competition is the oldest festival of its kind in Europe and one of the main attractions of the San Sebastian Summer Festival, Aste Nagusia, held during the week of 15 August. After admiring this amazing sight, tradition dictates that visitors and locals alike should enjoy a delicious ice cream in Los Italianos.

and new inventions, such as public street lighting (1899) and the new forms of travel.
Indeed, such vast numbers flocked to the city that, as mentioned in a document dated 1887, "the authorities were forced to ban cafés and other public establishments from closing at night in order to enable those that were unable to

La Concha, looking out towards Mount Igueldo and the Island of Santa Clara. Every 15 August, the San Sebastian track in Lasarte holds its biggest racing event of the year, the Gold Cup. Horseracing has been a permanent feature of the city's social calendar since 1916.

Main façade of the former Grand Casino, which since 1945 has been the headquarters of San Sebastian City Council. The ground floor houses the Central Library.

find accommodation in the city's hotels and residences or in the houses and buildings in the surroundings to spend the night there".

Three buildings capture the essence of this age of over-indulgence and frivolity: The Grand Casino – again a blend of the French style and the Spanish Renaissance – situated near Alderdi Eder and today home of the City Council, built in 1887 by the architects Morales de los Ríos and Aladrén; the Victoria Eugenia Theatre – built in the Spanish Neo-Renaissance and Neo-Plateresque styles and the work of Francisco de Urcola; and finally the Hotel María Cristina, –a fine example of international eclecticism, designed by Charles Mewes, commissioned to create a truly great hotel, "worthy of San Sebastian, with all the latest technical innovations on a par with the finest international establishments". Both the hotel and the theatre were opened in 1912 by Queen Maria Christina.

All these buildings played a part in creating the modern city. An irresistible combination of styles, forms and excesses, aesthetics and urban delights in keeping with the *Belle Époque*, all designed to form part of set on which to stage a tourism industry based on 'good taste' and impeccable style.

Reflecting the magnificence of a bygone era, the exclusive Hotel María Cristina, standing on the banks of the River Urumea on Paseo de la República Argentina, is the temporary home of the stars that visit San Sebastian each year during the International Film Festival. Famous guests include Leon Trotsky, Mata Hari, Maurice Ravel and Coco Chanel, to name but a few.

Right, the Victoria Eugenia Theatre, standing just a short distance from the Hotel María Cristina, which hosted the San Sebastian International Film Festival until 1999 and was refurbished in 2007, is one of the venues for the Musical Fortnight and the San Sebastian Jazz Festival, as well as countless dance and contemporary music events.

According to a text written in 1909, "foreigners visiting the city for the first time, despite having heard of its fame and reputation, will be amazed and overwhelmed. The streamlined elegance of its buildings, its spacious and harmonious proportions, its wide avenues and impeccable state of conservation and cleanliness give the impression of a pleasant, wealthy and healthy country.

It was precisely this pretended 'good taste' that characterised life in the spa city of San Sebastian that put Pío Baroja at odds with the town of his birth. Yet the same cannot be said for the land and the people that

La Zurriola Beach, in the district of Gros, was altered in 1994. It remains a firm favourite among the young, as it is ideal for surfing. On Zurriola Marítimo, the promenade that backs this beach, daytime restaurants and cafés become trendy clubs by night.

inhabited the coasts, an inextricable part of his seafaring legacy. "This sea along the Basque coasts", wrote Pío Baroja en *Las inquietudes de Shanti Andía*, "is amongst the wildest and most violent; it has sudden and unforeseen surges of rage; it is treacherous and shifting; it boils and trembles and is always rough and tumultuous". And in his memories he wrote: "I like the fact that I was born by the sea; to me it has always seemed to me a positive omen of freedom and change". On 14 September 1905, and influenced by the now tamed tides and the beneficial airs of the relaxed court

life of the early 20th century, in a letter to Benito Pérez Galdós thanking him for responding to a request for a recommendation, he wrote the following:

"Please forgive me for writing in such as rambling and disjointed manner, but with these banal airs and the dull and vegetative life of San Sebastian, where vanity is the only form of intellect, the mind becomes dim".

In addition to this exasperating 'good taste', the city also all too often fell victim to the stupidity of its public authorities, more concerned with putting a shine on its 'little Paris' than with the bust of Victor Hugo on display in his House Museum in Pasajes. That "great, universally-renowned poet, who has spoken well of the Basques on numerous occasions"... "A poet", concluded Baroja, "is mere small fry for a councillor of San Sebastian. If only he had been a Gentleman of the Bedchamber! Or at least held a minor title!".

A second casino, the ornate Kursaal, was built in 1922 to save the upper classes from suffering the unpleasant overcrowding of the first. The ban on gaming imposed by Primo de Rivera marked a turning point in the influx of tourists. "Revenue", wrote Sánchez Mazas in the early 1930s, "is not flowing quite so fast as before. Now it comes from a wider number of less volatile sources, earned through hard work and perhaps even greater...the rise in the number of delightful holidaymakers from Aragón alone brings in as much as countless evenings of roulette".

The San Sebastian International Film Festival is one of the city's greatest cultural events. Now in its 58th year, its greatest successes include, apart from the Gold Shell awarded to the best film, the Donostia Award in recognition of a film career, and the Zabaltegi Section, for new and unclassifiable directors.

Today, the site where the casino once stood is occupied by a striking architectural complex that projects the city's vision of its own future. Known locally as the *Cubos del Kursaal* or 'Kursaal Cubes', it houses the Convention Centre, two auditoriums and an exhibition hall. This minimalist design, the work of Rafael Moneo, was conceived as "two stranded rocks" embedded at the mouth of the Urumea facing Zurriola Beach. It opened in 1999 and hosts the main events included in San Sebastian's International Film Festival. The Victoria Eugenia Theatre was the original venue for this festival, which was started in 1953.
The city's leisure facilities also include the Paseo Nuevo or 'New Promenade' (1914-1919), "built", as the plans for the project state, "with the sole object of providing a place of recreation for the countless visitors to the city. It is therefore an ornate and elaborate project whose principal characteristic must lie in its appeal and attractiveness". The promenade runs along the seafront around the base of Mount Urgull, from

the mouth of the Urumea as far as the Aquarium – opened in 1928 and recently remodelled, this was Spain's very first natural science museum –, situated near the fishing harbour. On the final stretch of the promenade, the sculpture entitled *Construcción vacía* (Empty Structure, 2002), by Jorge Oteiza, presides over the start of the bay. On the other side, at the far end of Ondarreta Beach stands the *El peine del viento* (The Wind Comb, 1976), the work of sculptor Eduardo Chillida and architect Luis Peña Ganchegui, who also designed Plaza de la Trinidad, a space for country sports and the spectacular venue for 'Jazzaldia', San Sebastian's Jazz Festival.

The Aquarium-Sea Palace guarantees a fascinating voyage of discovery into the depths of the ocean. Children will be enthralled throughout the tour. The skeleton of the last whale caught on the coasts of Guipúzcoa in 1878 and an acrylic 360° tunnel taking visitors past sharks and rays are just a couple of the attractions on offer.

Above, Plaza de la Trinidad, the most eye-catching and welcoming venue for Jazzaldia.

Nature has been a constant theme in Basque art. Extensive aesthetic discourse into the concepts of the vacuum, matter and the occupancy and clearing of space has led to superb poetic expressions of immense beauty and significance.

Left, Empty structure *(Jorge Oteiza). Below,* The Wind Comb *(Eduardo Chillida).*

A number of other architectural styles have also gradually shaped the city and its skyline. The Modernist style with its elaborate *art nouveau* decoration can be seen in a number of buildings on Calle Prim, the work of architect Luis Elizalde. The building housing the Royal Yacht Club (José Manuel Aizpúrua and Joaquín Labayen, 1929), and the Equitativa building (Fernando Arzadun, 1933), in Gros, are fine examples of the Rationalist style. This is the modern city, full of attractions and sights that further enhance the appeal of contemporary San Sebastian. Corners, streets and promenades that are ideal for quiet contemplation and a solitary stroll, or for mingling with the crowds on avenues and in the bars and taverns, many of which are authentic museums showcasing miniature culinary delights. A city which Hemingway cleverly identified as a good place to get to grips with oneself, before getting down to some serious fun. He saw Donostia as a charming city, and one of the most delightful places in Europe.

At the end of La Concha Bay, next to the City Hall, stands the Royal Yacht Club, reminiscent of a boat that has run aground.

THE CITY AND ITS ARTISTS

In addition to the sculptures by Oteiza and Chillida mentioned above, visitors to the city can also admire the *Pietá* (1999) on the wall of the Church of San Vicente in the Old Quarter, the work of Oteiza and José Ramón Anda. A mural in memory of the musician Father Donostia, situated in the hall of the Banco Guipuzcoano building, is the other public work created by the Orio-born sculptor Jorge Oteiza.

Eduardo Chillida's love of the city is reflected in works such as *Homenaje a Fleming* (A Tribute to Fleming, 1955), on Paseo de La Concha; *Besarkada* (The Embrace, 1994) and a tribute to Rafael Ruiz Balerdi–, at the Pico del Loro; *Homenaje a Pedro Arana* (A Tribute to Pedro Arana, 1963), on Mount Urgull; *Bakearen Gurutzea* (The Cross of Peace, 1997), on the portico of the Cathedral of El Buen Pastor; and the Chillida-Leku Museum, in Zabalaga House on the outskirts of San Sebastian.

Works by other Basque artists can also be seen in and around the city.

Examples include Augustín Ibarrola's *Estela* (Trail, 1988) situated in the docks, and one of twelve identical works that look out to sea from the ports and harbours of the Basque Country; or *Las Siluetas* (Silhouettes, 1992) and *Juego de niños* (Child's Play, 1991), in the district of Intxaurrondo. This district is also the site of a work by the *Equipo 57* – a group that opposed subjectivism and surrealism – originally set up by Oteiza and made up of numerous Basque artists including Ibarrola and Basterretxea until its disappearance in 1961–, as well as the sculptures entitled *Monolito* (Monolith) and *Formas en crecimiento* (Growing forms, 1994), by Koldobika Jáuregui.

The sculpture entitled *Herri txistu otza* (1975) by Remigio Mendiburi, is situated on the façade of the first building on Avenida de la Libertad. Other works by this artist include his mural entitled *Escultura* (Sculpture, 1973), in the district of Amara; and the series featuring the sculptures entitled *Ruido del*

abismo, *Noche* y *Viento del abismo* (Noise from the Abyss, Night and Wind from the Abyss, 1977), situated in the central offices of the Kutxa savings bank on Garibay Street.
Ricardo Ugarte created *Estela* (Trail, 1969), which can be seen in the District of Amara, as well as *Escultura* (Sculpture, 1972) and *Gaztelu* (1994), both situated in Miramón.
Néstor Basterretxea sculpted *Homenaje al coreógrafo Iztueta* (Tribute to the Choreographer Iztueta, 1967), situated in the district of Gros, as well as *Paloma de la Paz* (Dove of Peace, 1988), in Plaza Padre Donostia in Amara; and the *Monumento a Pío Baroja* (Monument to Pío Baroja, 1971), in El Antiguo.
José Ramón Anda created *Zeharki* (Through, 1982), situated in Ondarreta Gardens, on the site of the former prison and replacing the monument in memory of the residents of San Sebastian that died whilst fighting alongside Franco.
The university campus is the site of a work by Andrés Nagel known as *Sin título* (Untitled, 1992).
Another magnificent sculpture, creating a setting worthy of a picture postcard, forms a major landmark on the cityscape. At the top of Mount Urgull, perched on top of a chapel rising up above La Mota Castle, the magnificent *Sagrado Corazón* (Sacred Heart), reflecting the official aesthetics of the time, has kept watch over the city since 1950. It is the work of Federico Coullaut, a sculptor known for the religious figures he created for the Easter processions.
An image that is permanently etched in the minds of permanent and temporary residents in the city alike, is that of the railings along the Paseo de la Concha promenade. Together with La Perla (1912), the spa hotel situated on the same promenade, the railings, designed by Juan Rafael Alday in 1910, form one of the city's most famous landmarks and the defining hallmark of the city designed for rest, recreation and leisure conceived by Goicoa.
The railings along La Concha promenade, a symbol of the advertising slogans proclaiming "the world's finest and busiest beach", "the Pearl of the Cantabrian, the perfect beach", singly sums up everything San Sebastian expected of itself. Even film director Frank Borzage was unable to resist its charms during the

63

Donostia-San Sebastian

A Tribute to Fleming, *a granite sculpture by Eduardo Chillida, today standing on La Concha Promenade, has been displayed in various locations around the city.*

Like portholes, the famous railings that line La Concha Promenade are an invitation to gaze at the delights of this bay.

filming of the 1936 movie 'Desire' when the railings managed to briefly steal the limelight from other world famous icons such as Marlene Dietrich and Gary Cooper.

In contrast to the picture postcard images used to promote San Sebastian, writers and poets such as José María Salaverría, Gabriel Celaya or Azorín have put forward alternative symbols more in keeping with the essence of a city that faces the sea. Examples include the seagull – "majestic and enigmatic... Seagulls are the doves of the sea, but less fortunate. Wild and free, they are the messengers that announce an approaching storm". This image appears to be more in keeping with the timeless natural images of a city swept by the strong north-westerly winds and which, as Salaverría wrote, has far more character, style and history than that of the veneer of courtly habits that stripped San Sebastian of its "intense flavour of gullible originality".

"The seagulls have accompanied me", wrote Celaya, "on my walks along the Urumea, on the beach and all along the coast".

In several of his chronicles, Azorín also referred to the city's seafaring nature, and the sense of discovery and the capacity for appeasement of this unique pavilion of repose looking out over the ocean.

"In this beautiful city, next to the sea, it seems as though we must have forgotten something; we are filled with the instinctive suspicion that such a sense of quiet is only possible through some form of sacrifice: Perhaps a momentary sacrifice of love for the blue, for transparency, for distant clarity. Our inner self is unable to decide whether we prefer clear or undefined boundaries, deep tones or subtle shades. Yet in the much-loved city, we strive to create harmony through synthesis: We have the sea surrounding La Concha Bay with its fine, elegant lines; from Paseo Nuevo we can see the vast expanse of the Atlantic Ocean, as we slowly make our way up to Urgull, passing by the ancient fortifications which give us a fleeting sense of history, before suddenly coming face to face with the immenseness of the sea; the symbol of eternity. At the foot of the hill the sea is green, glaucous; in the distance it is a steely grey, cerulean; the tones shift and change with the clouds and light. A flock of seagulls fly overhead, soaring and dipping, turning this way and that. The seagull, with its motionless wings outstretched, swoops and soars, crying out joyfully at each turn. We are seated on a smooth white stone, next to a small, puny tree, bent double by the relentless winds".

Today San Sebastian has cleverly resolved to put its past as a spa city and resort behind it, determining to embark on a different style of city life, more in keeping with the present times. Hence its candidacy for the 2016 European City of Culture, its commitment to becoming a world-renowned international centre for research in Science and Technology (The Donostia International Physics Centre) or its tireless quest to take its culinary know-how from the very finest restaurants to the heights of skill and knowledge through the University of Mondragón's Basque Culinary Centre.

The photo shows Elena Arzak, Pedro Subijana, Juan Mari Arzak, Martín Berasategui and Hilario Arbelaitz at the San Sebastian Gastronomy Congress. Together with Karlos Arguiñano and Andoni Luis Aduriz, they represent the greatest innovators and the finest ambassadors of Basque cuisine.